HOW *to* PROVE *a* THEORY

HOW *to* PROVE *a* THEORY

NICOLE TONG

Washington Writers' Publishing House
Washington, D.C.

COVER PAINTING by John Kelly
COVER DESIGN by Meg Reid
BOOK DESIGN by Barbara Shaw

Library of Congress Cataloging-in-Publication Data
Names: Tong, Nicole, 1979- author.
Title: How to prove a theory / Nicole Tong.
Description: Washington, DC : Washington Writers' Publishing House, 2017. |
    Includes bibliographical references.
Identifiers: LCCN 2017029466 | ISBN 9781941551134 (pbk.)
Classification: LCC PS3620.O5826 A6 2017 | DDC 811/.6—dc23
LC record available at https://lccn.loc.gov/2017029466

Printed in the United States of America

WASHINGTON WRITERS' PUBLISHING HOUSE
P. O. Box 15271
Washington, DC 20003

for my parents

CONTENTS

III.

RESTITUTION FOR CHAOS

Before Earth, its urgency. Before that, the possibility of sound.
   The sea? Well that is something else entirely.

***

As a child, I was easily frightened. Solitude offered little reprieve.
   It's just the wind. It's the just wind.

***

To solemnize the quiet would be too easy.
   I search the grottos for intruders; they remain an empty darkness.

***

Things are out of place, and that is cause for comfort.
   The crow's nest at the top of a tree isn't strange to me.

***

Before the long tunneling cave through which the world bends, light.
   Before its promise, I couldn't help but breathe.

SISTER

Forget about smoking weed
       with soccer players in the woods
              near the Methodist church

while I said Hail Marys
       and kept watch. Shifted my weight from hip
              to hip as if to ask, *Is this attractive?*

Waited for feedback
       from the shadows. *Forget Mom and Dad,*
              you'd say. *They're some kind of crazy.*

We repacked bags with the seasons.
       Buried them in the backs of our closets.
              Clothing and essentials in case.

Thought one morning I'd find you
       long gone since
              ours was a house of exits.

But when, in my sixteenth year, you watched
       my slight frame get smaller
              as the car pulled away

from the boarding school parking lot,
       I knew what you knew: the difference
              between not speaking and letting something go

unspoken. Between what actually happened
     and the mythologies we tell our husbands decades
          later. We say, *Mom wigged out.* We don't say

the institution's name. We can't say,
     That was the year we saw Dad pull the trigger.
     I said, You're such a bitch

when I meant *Remember.*
     You were there.
         You walked beside me each day.

Let white light erase
the landscape until all
becomes snow or scrimshaw.

The present always wants
another passing between
worlds: more

than living and—
My body composes
its own sentence.

Tentatively starts
and stops. *Stop
down:* to allow less

light. Which is to say
gravity. There are ways
to contain a thing

without binding it
in twine.

IN OFFICE HOURS MY STUDENT, BACK FROM WAR, EXPLAINS

why he would like me to announce *Lights*
before I turn them on or off. Tells me
about his job in artillery. All semester,
construction rattles our room: sometimes
it's a drill, others a jackhammer. Each time
Robert reacts viscerally, carries the echo
of war in his shoulders, the furrow of his brow.
In small groups students work. One taps
a pencil as he thinks. Robert becomes a cyclone,
its sharpening point. I consider pressing the button
classrooms have in common with convenience stores.
Instead I order Robert out of the room. Months before,
when the Home Depot manager asked how he handled
a challenge at his last position during the interview,
Robert responded before throwing the man's stapler
at his face: *What the fuck do you want me to say?*

HYPOTHESIS

sealed shut   unable
to let anything in
out   what was there to say

each thing in its place
didn't   I mention this
because I can   I am

not there   theirs
is a story I tell

NOCEBO THEORY

The man died in his sleep despite the clock,
its alarm, ringing for years, thirty minutes
to the hour for fear of this very scenario:

death by sleep. When he looked for a bride
half a decade ago, before he made this country
home, he went out to the fields. He let tall grasses

brush his hips until she was found. And when
he took her in his arms for the first time, he asked
if she could start a stopped heart. He wanted in a wife,

life. But before that, he set a clock and lived
by its turning. Each degree its own landscape
of turning: hours moving toward an X's

top half, leaves giving their colors back
to the ground, a girl walking down a path
turns around as if something's been forgotten.

Expect no call for a rune or cure. It is not a spirit
but something else that's to blame. This is just to say
that men die every day for reasons in their dreams.

NO THEORY

I.

My mother packs two suitcases
  On my behalf straps me
    Into the front seat

As if I were a child
  Two hours into the trip home
    My hand reaches for the radio dial

Tries to build a haven of noise
  In college a girl learns conviction
    Learns to call her peers *women*

In stark contrast
  To the way I see myself
    Age seven

Still in the mirror
  Of the kerosene heater
    Blue nightgown with a gentle pattern

Of flowers my small frame
  Leading up to neck
    It was the middle of the night

The machine's heat pushed
  Against me
    Certainly my body

Was the calm
        That made requests quietly
                So as not to cause alarm

II.

My first kiss was from a girl
        With curly hair
                Can't remember

Her name I remember
        Getting ready for a dance recital
                From the communal bathroom

Of the shelter for women and children
        The sheen of tights against the back
                Of my thighs

Believing that
        Kiss aged me
                It's spring again

The collegiate mind hinges
        On facts
                Though my jaw would not

Unlock itself *no*
        Surely made its way out
                Of my mouth not once

But twice
  This is not the way
    I replay it happening

This is the way
  That word lives
    Daily I choose

To practice it
  Or to leave it behind

HYPOTHESIS

at an aperture a way in too

I prefer moving out of around

anything but   staring a thing down

directly watching it (disappear)

calling it   by name

PINK PILL THEORY

What piled up piled up
gradually. I kept steady count.

I did not need much. I did so
regularly. Practice clouded the view.

Making it difficult to distinguish
things seen from *things seem*.

INACCURATE THEORY

There is a girl and an otherwise
abandoned forest in which the girl
counts backward from thirty.

Leaves resist falling. The hum around her,
the applause of blackbird wings. Light
finds an opening.

In this place, she is her own
collapse. It's not like the dark
room where a world hangs

in the waiting and becomes.
It's the instant where all is almost—
and lost. A leading chord fades.

A sigh ruptures silence.
Shiva summons the landscape
in slow motion. She counts to calm

flocks of birds. When the wind
won't take, there's no need
to tether self to shore.

WISTFUL THEORY

Johnson, Vermont

No hopeless field nearby, no whisper
moving through the body's hull.

Today, silence. Even emptiness
yearns for something.

Today, a steep walk, my face lashed
by wind and snow. The bivouac of birds undone,

replaced by milkweed's collapsed casket.
The moment before this landscape's erasure

will be a prophetic sigh. No, it
will be the stillness of water's fine lie.

AND THE PLACE WAS WATER

After Lorine Niedecker

In the calm of morning
        Gulls wrestle
                Clams from shells
        Their beaks
Steep in muddy pools on shore

I was born just west
        Of here
                Dad went to sea
        While mom ate grape jelly
Left enough food

For her children
        I remember the pine's sigh
                In winter
        Cicadas loosening selves
From selves

By summer
        I picked tomatoes
                Though small
        And under-ripe
Made mud pies

With Grandmother's spoons
        Dad fixed
                Helicopters
        For the military
Kept hobbies

To the weekends
        And once bought a car
                For a woman
        He never knew
They kept us afloat

We went to mass
        Said prayers
                When Dad was home
        Our prayers changed
Semper Fi do or die!

Or *Goodnight Chesty Puller*
        Wherever you are
                Wherever you are in town
        You're in a place
Built on water

Bittersweet
     Is the slip
          From here
     The anchors
Too few

This year
     No floods near
          Fall was fraught
     With leaves changing
Dad's side

Went numb post-stroke
     Doctors asked him to walk
          On legs of water
     So he did
Without question

I am not the flood
     I do not want to be
          Make me a river
     (Fast as you can)
But let me keep my name

The hush
      Of it over dusk
            While gulls fly
      To sea
Here has never been

So lovely a plea
      Leave the new
            Unbought water
      This never-the-same
Place of mine

SELF-PORTRAIT AS VENUS

After Sandro Botticelli

Oh, so this is the world?
Wind gods blowing over-

due vowels with rounding mouths.
Sky above, sea beneath, and I

am between. This is the world
divided: two people

with different wants.
One places delicate detail

of petals, narrates stories
always already in star. The other

moves the tide that rises, promises
to swallow me whole.

II

———

THEORY FOR THE LIVING

After Monica Cook

My skirt bursts into cloud.
Some birds fly away and take with them

the land's color. For decades, I imagine
everything is left to age and ash.

This is not the work of weather.
Grief is a color you can't see through,

can never quite get to divisions of things.
Wasn't I present to close the barn door?

How did need escape me? Wasn't there always
milk in the air, covering remains

until nothing died anymore? Won't the crows
come back? Didn't the others come to our aid?

Couldn't the maps save us? Tell us where?
Was this the first time I was shattered,

remade as the still of snapshot?
I can't say why some birds didn't fly.

Can't name one good reason
for which things stay.

CHINOOK THEORY

Having made gravel a kind of home
for sixty miles of footwork I imagine

my father alive each time the Park Police helicopter circles
the Potomac beside the towpath. Imagine how measured

the cargo when he operated a twin-engined monster
(in the 70s his silence not a *soldier's heart* but *shell shock*).

Near a Marine base in North Carolina my nephew monitors
weather on this side of the mountains. He texts when he suspects

changing trail conditions. *Careful, Nicole, a chinook*
may be coming by which he means wind. But such a coincidence

is not geographically precise on this Appalachian stretch,
a country away from the correct coast. A year since

I spent hours plucking feathers from a hospice bed
were it possible to construct a bird to rise up and greet the dead.

GRIEF THEORY

For Anna Bess Williams

Grief wakes me, insists I play your voicemails
in the bathroom in the middle of the night.

I think I hear your name each time I shop
for produce. All spring, the figure running

in front of me for twenty miles
is Grief. Just as it stops for water (finally

human-like), I pass it with a sense of satisfaction only to beg it
back when it vanishes. Last week a friend told me her daughter

beat the pillow where the child's father once lay for hours
after *his Savior called him home.* Hers is the kind of longing

I have come to understand. For six months, I have
gotten used to the space you made between this world

and the next. Your mother tells me she remembers best
the days following delivery when you found rest

in her arms alone in the middle of a blizzard that kept
visitors at bay. Today wind claimed the letter I wrote you

the day your daughter was born, five days
before you died. That night, I drank wine, offered

a toast to you and the fragile heart that kept
going despite your doctor's fears. Even now,

Grief reminds me of the silence behind the curtain
in your hospital room. The plaster casts of your hands

your children will live to fill. A curl
cut from your hair gently unraveling.

SELF-PORTRAIT AS DAUGHTER

The only time I've held a gun,
I stood in the woods of western Carolina
with Anna's father the summer

following her death. I gathered stories
for her mother. Put on a Storm Trooper mask
barely big enough for my head for the amusement

of her son. Agreed to a lesson in country living
without changing my blue silk shift and purple
Mizunos for Joe. Surprising was the Remington's

weight, the .22. My target, a twin gallon bucket box
and the number two he invited me to kill before the first
fired bullet pierced the cardboard with a certainty

like death. Joe collected the shell
while I examined the digit's hollowed hook.
Three times today I have passed the folded flag

a soldier delivered at my own father's funeral.
Two salute shells. One small black matte urn
of his ashes my mother wanted for me. I recall

the echo of the rifles' final round so much
like my father: the volley I could feel coming, still
reason enough to flinch.

GENTLE OBSESSIONS

After Emily Dickinson

When I folded the memory
of your death into an accordion shape

and tossed it to sea, I was certain it would play
a hymn like the ones you loved. And you were right:

the soul knows how to sustain itself
despite submersion, to give up the land's edge

lost to the flood until everything is the horizon.
When you said spring leaves only water

whole, did you mean the sky and ocean are
windows? When nothing can be tethered

to shore by phone line or otherwise,
which practices survive?

PREDILECTION

Down gravel roads
  back in Jacksonville, there's a renaissance
of domestic cats— nebulous green irises—
  a fretful speech of yowls, owls answer oh yes
a price is paid

for preferences—
  the way cats fashion their tails at angles
the way the farmer paves his road with little stones
  the way I like my uniform pressed with starch
  that smells of spring.

Even scent is
  a thing, an ordinary object
residing on a nightstand: a brush, a votive
  candle, a poem's page, gutters of books marked
with strands of brown

hair like coffee
  stains. I write today prepared to explain
my partiality for constructing syll-
  ables, reaching lines, a word hushed, _pre-
dilection._ I

too dislike an
 adverse book of verse, a poet lacking
the literal imagination, a mind of
 possibility, a make-believe place for
the genuine.

LET THE DEAD BURY THEIR OWN

I.

The facts are troubling. Scientists
conduct mortality studies on Marines

who drank contaminated water for decades.
Results are said to be *forthcoming*.

Online base news items include
only prematurely warm weather warnings

and a traffic advisory. A disciple
asked Jesus for leave upon a familial death

and heard this reply: *Let the dead
bury their own dead.*

II.

After he died of B-Cell leukemia, after Agent Orange
took what it could, after the well closed, after the
shots of pure gold administered in Quantico, four
years after the government deemed him disabled,
after the dehumanizing synecdoche, *boots on the
ground,* to describe the next generation of soldiers
as if their very bodies are disposable

                                    Civilians ask
whether my father's funeral featured a 21- gun
salute. Servicemen know the difference between
salutes and volleys, which don't come from guns but
rather rifles. This battlefield custom began so the
dead could be collected. One side sent two shots to
cease hostilities, another to resume. They called it *A
Salute to the Union.*

III.

The first person I ever knew to be cremated
taught a sixth-grade gym class. He ran laps

alongside me as I took asthmatic gasps. Said
Foreman, you need to move. In my father's

speech, I said he needed to *simmer down*.
After all, he was not a Marine anymore

and we were only eleven. We couldn't
have known was what was happening

inside of him. Cells growing in marrow
until his body had to fight the blood

that fed it. By the end, did he wish
for wind to erase him?

IV.

Baby Heaven: the section of Jacksonville's City
Cemetery occupied by those who did not live
past childhood because of the water they drank
from hoses in those humid Carolina summers
of the 70s when bathwater did the throwing.
Because their mothers, ever-thirsty as they grew
in utero, couldn't have known. Because effects
are generational, female survivors should expect
infertility, miscarriages, and stillbirths. Search for
Baby Heaven, and you'll find images of playgrounds,
retail spaces flooded with pink and blue, headbands
adorned with handmade flowers rather than rows
of headstones marking a lost generation.

GENERATIONAL MEMORY THEORY

When she finds herself apologizing
to the daughter she doesn't have,

it is because scientists found
mice trained to avoid a scent

as sweet as cherry blossoms
passed down the anxiety

its sweetness induced
for two generations, which proves

the mice's *offspring and its after that*
would avoid the scent, despite

never having experienced that sweetness.
When she asks why her body

hasn't let her have children,
don't tell her God has a reason.

Tell her you're sorry you didn't know
what to do with the fear of the man

who was her father, for the smell
of whiskey and turpentine

he could never wash from his hands
so that when he touched you

there was something toxic
about it every goddamn time.

HOW TO APOLOGIZE

After Satellite AEHF-1 or the Course Corrections of Conception

Speak kindly. Ask what you've done

to create distance. When you get an answer,

follow up with something like *This is a delicate situation.*

or, *I can see I'm going to have to do something differently.*

After acknowledging a problem, discuss potential consequences.

To save anything, you must risk its loss. In this instance,

interventions numbered in the hundreds. Slowly, she came around

with her sophisticated strut, a trajectory

that demonstrated what she had to offer.

HYPOTHESIS

water rose
I caught whole
decades of our lives
in the act

PENTIMENTO

My city is a hotbed
of newly fallen crows

whose musculatures
magnet to sidewalks.

They unfurl themselves
into carbon dying.

Before crows, magnolia petals
and the slow mechanics

of my wound
body. Is this the way history goes:

a solitary turn to make sense
of the litany of things

left? Before the scene read
Things lost to a flood, maybe

it was the simple revelry
of rising water. Was there joy,

a rare laughter, the enviable
task of sharing without worry

of anchor? *Rain fell
in an empty town.*

That doesn't mean I was
some frail, ghastly flower.

What we knew of morning,
we knew with certainty.

What does the earth sink into?
Its weight. Once we're gone,

who answers for this urging
to pair things: One, two?

Before the birds, no wall
of glass or forecast

of broken operations.
No calculus, cartography,

or sky gone
dark. Still my city stops

at an aftermath of *could be.*
Strange summations beginning

with *crow.* Count backward
with *bone* and *age.* Given

the practice to call things gone,
how shall I speak of the line,

which neatly remains?

HYPOTHESIS

chair   chest   bed   wall

ghost   forms   ghost

narratives taking over some

thing the dead once wore

III

SOME THEORY

I go for days. Find nothing
worthy to wish on: this crow
smashed to bone

on a sidewalk, those flayed feathers—
a makeshift weather vane.
In each direction, I see

reminders that each thing suffers
from placelessness and wants
to be a bird. When I was young

I wore a bra overnight
in case of a fire. Suitcase packed
included encyclopedia volume E-

tap shoes, yellow yarn scarf,
enough enough
that some got away.

INTERIOR WITH SUDDEN JOY

Las Vegas, Nevada

Though we are young and poor,
we're a far cry from needing to heed

my father's cross-country moving advice:
Take my camper and park it

at some Walmart till you get your shit straight.
A uniformed man delivers our first bed. I peer

at the peephole-distorted figure of him.
Suppose happiness waits like finish lines

around every street corner
ubiquitous as escort flyers

twelve-year-olds binge on
while waiting for the school bus.

Instead of the heat, we complain
about a lack of sweet tea.

What night takes, morning returns.
We accrue what's ours an item at a time:

shower curtain, dishwashing liquid, found
five-dollar poker chip. I ask questions

for the sake of it, gratified each time
someone answers.

INTIMACY THEORY

For John

In light of the river, the way it turns.
First a gathering of ice. Then snow

building a false start of the river's edge.
Tell me what's empirical: winter at my back

all season, snow turns to rain in my hair.
Tell me how many times today my body has

worked against itself. Thinking of you is
something like breath. A slow release of time

built up in my mouth. When there are no words,
no idiom will do: *tie the knot, tie one on,*

cut ties, tongue-tied. You are anything
but an obstruction. You are everything

if not each moment before. O
transitivity. O verb waiting to be.

MARATHON

Always a world at the edge
        Of a gatehouse
                Always syntax

A password
        I'm between idioms
                For *family*

Home a kind of heaven
        I search for
                There are markers

On birch trees
        Their paper skins
                Seem to spell
And dispel
        It's not lonely along the way

                ***

Sheets on a clothesline
      Silhouette a woman
            Wind moves her outline closer

Then farther from me
      The sun is on her side
            Always small towns on the way

Always a place waiting
      For a name I go
            Here is not home

But I recognize the sounds
      A bus passes
            Gravel litters a paved road

Kids holler from windows
      We're almost there!
            As they point at the town's edge

And examine what it isn't

     ***

I might not follow
       Brick sidewalks
              Leading to towns

I've known well
       I might run the line
              Of the river

That also knows
       My name
              Traces a way

Through tangles
       Of branches
              Washed ashore

What I fear most
       Isn't the current

    ***

I'll say it now
        I've never known the truth
                About stars

Never known why they hide
        I confess
                It pleases me

For a moment the terror
        Of birds
                Banners the sky

Dusk sets in
        Starting with my eyes
                What I look for changes

And what I rely on
        That changes also
                An array of objects still

In the making
        A river's spine
                A rising tide

        ***

The sea covering
     And recovering
          What can't be

Destroyed
     The past
          I've given up

For now
     The wind blows
          It doesn't

Stop for me

CORPOREAL THEORIES

I. CALL

In your absence
(my body, mine)
there were shoes, bottles, gauze

in a bathroom cabinet
        needle taking over: ~~need~~

bruise, suture, scuff
        on the counter of a shoe

all imply something ~~was~~
done. ~~What once~~
~~was.~~

II. RESPONSE

Where wound and white space are
the same ~~name~~, explanations
become stitches

      I stand on.

You're nearly visible
through my skin ~~as if silenced~~ there

      (in a square torso).

Come

      words. ~~I sew~~
      ~~them.~~ This way.

MATERNAL THEORY

Following each low-wage paycheck
I buy one outfit for a baby I don't have, a girl

I would call Lily. There are onesies, holiday
shirts, sweaters smocked with the cutest animals

in the kingdom. *It's unlucky to want something
so badly,* scolds a friend who offers me charms

for the superstitious and freshly roasted coffee
to counter my practice. I give up

running. Try willing my once-asthmatic body
into womb. I store tiny clothes under the bed,

sleep soundly on top of them as if whispering
a wish into fruition. Years and years I wait

for Lily to announce herself
like the trumpet of her namesake.

HYPOTHESIS

The way wounds are
fixed. Words become
maps. Become
backbone or railroad
tracks.

MISCARRIAGE AS A LANDLINE PHONE CALL

For J-

What I meant to say
became this desert, a song
I know, a tune I try

to hum over rain
and dial tone (this call
over). I am pressed

to a receiver. Night
falls. Fails me every time.
Never listens. Back

home, gravel roads take
unexpected turns. Lead
nowhere. I was content

with this. I am unsure
when words began to matter,
the first time I was speech-

less. Some stories are not mine
to tell. Others belong to no one
else. The accessory

for my first school play
was a cane that could not hold
my weight. I learned the hard way.

Once went down Kroger aisles
reciting times tables so fast
I puked in frozen foods. Tonight

I remind myself the sea is real.
I know because I've seen waves
lap the shore. Still the distance

between us is one I can't see,
the way deserts erase names
from tombstones engraved *Dear.*

I'll hold. The drone
on the other end isn't shrill
and it keeps me.

FULL AS OPERA

Before first light strikes the windshield
and you are stirred into waking. Before

the caw of crows. Before animals
knew to move through the forest—

dank and dark, you had a vision:
there was a girl in a conflagration

of branch of ash. She wore a straw hat.
Her dress said she lived in some *ago*.

When she was nervous, she spun
her whole body to collapse:

her bones giving out, birds protesting
above, clouds erasing stories

in the stars. Always she lived with this
suspense, the way time separates

itself from place until—
There she is, suspended

again, displaced by tense
shifts and wandering vowels:

her mouth seems between sounds.
And she spins, as though in spinning

she could name Night
some round word like *Found*.

OVERLEVERAGED THEORY

I'd call you by name. I'd say, *Mi*—
but the sea is too wide

this lifetime. I'd say
vehicles matter most. I'd say

the way to safety is concrete
with things: twine, a receding tide,

a could-be continent of islands
punctuating what's beneath. Imagine

heaven a fairytale reversing itself:
ducks gather above, darkness below

erases the boots on your feet. Our house
becomes a boat on its side.

The dancing and music stop long after
your last reply. I'm left with this

fragment of alphabet, the V our arms make
with you on my back. I know

neither how to hold you up nor where
to safely place you down.

This process called trust
keeps happening.

HYPOTHESIS

I'm so alive
I leave you
shaking. In my boots
the soles lie. I remove them.
Run through what's hollow.

THOUGHTS BEFORE SELF-PORTRAIT

After Alice Neel

Daughter born. Left Cuba. Daughter
died. Recovered *I* and kept going.
Doing little destroys all that's left.

Nobody owns
O the shape,
the sound. Hollow

in my mouth:
a space that can't be-
come anyone.

HOW TO PROVE A THEORY

For John

And on our second date you told the story
of your family in China, which you began

in jest, *I have to have a son.* You moved
food around your plate. Shared how your father,

the second born, felt birth order made his choices
less consequential until his older brother,

the opera star, died of an appendicitis. How familial
attention shifted to him as if the singer

had never lived to intone a note. After, your father
became a Catholic priest in part because the vows

disallowed the children expected of him
as the only living son. Later, Communists came,

held your grandfather captive, and demanded ransom
before taking the family home. The priest boarded

the last flight out of Beijing to San Francisco,
asylum granted, before settling in D.C. where he met

your mother, renounced his vows, fell in love,
and fathered two sons. *But you have a brother!*

I shouted as if problem-solving because then
you did. I loved you before the doctor's warning,

Things with your brother are dire. Before Paul's
final night when you spoke slowly as morphine's drip.

To prove a theory of the beauty of this world,
acknowledge its cruelty: the brother lacking children

is less likely to be given a new heart so he's fated
to spend two years choking as if drowning but remains

thankful for each night he falls asleep with his head
in your lap, for the bandages we wrap at the ankles

once edema takes hold. That night, you told me
your grandfather died before he got word your father

was a father, despite such an unlikelihood.
Then, when you were eleven you watched as *his* heart

stopped in front of you. You were sent to school
later that afternoon. It was April Fool's Day. When

you told people your dad was dead, few believed you.
To prove a theory of fragility, you will master capacity:

to fill hallowed air with laughter, even after the hardest day
with the help of a book titled *Terribly Offensive Jokes*

Volume I, discovering seven more in the set, recalling
Paul tell each line as if his own. And before you lead

our way home, you will pretend to drop the ashes
that had been his body as Paul would have done

to you. For a second, your lineage suspended,
its weight contained. And yet these generations are

mirrors for looking into. Only you remain. And yet.

DEAD RECKONING

To figure out where you'll end up,
speed, time and course must remain steady.
There were logs. Charts, compasses

and clocks. For a time, there was no sky.
I had to forget the sky was there,
which was not an easy task given the facts:

the birds *did* fly. They *did* land on the deck.
Given a dilated eye. The pool of the sea at night
that surely reflected something.

NOTES

In "Restitution for Chaos" the term "crow's nest" is a nautical term for "the platform of shelter for lookout near the top of the mast."

"In Office Hours My Student, Back from War, Explains" makes reference to the panic buttons added to telephones in public classrooms after the Virginia Tech shooting in 2007.

The 2005 Doris Salcedo installation *Atrabiliarios* at SFMOMA prompted the "Hypothesis" poems as well as "Corporeal Theories." I am so grateful to this artist for helping me consider communal loss and its generational impacts.

"Nocebo Theory" dramatizes Alexis Madrigil's 2011 article "The Dark Side of the Placebo Effect: When Intense Belief Kills." It describes Sudden Unexpected Nocturnal Death Syndrome in Hmong immigrants to the United States.

Sally Mann's photo "Shiva at Whistle Creek" inspired "Inaccurate Theory."

"And the Place Was Water" is the epigraph for Lorine Niedecker's "Paean to Place." Variations of the lines "They kept us/ afloat" were written in light of Niedecker's constructions in this same vein. Chesty Puller was the most decorated Marine in U.S. history. The italicized portions in the final stanza appear in the final stanza of Niedecker's poem.

The figure from a 2005 untitled painting by Monica Cook is dramatized in "Theory for the Living." Another untitled work ("With Mallards") by this artist is the seed for "Overleveraged Theory."

"Chinook" refers to Boeing's CH-47 tandem rotor helicopter named after the Chinook Indian Nation and is a weather phenomenon that creates a warm moving wind.

"Predilection" is a reflection on the original version of Marianne Moore's poem, "Poetry." Jacksonville refers to a town in North Carolina. I am grateful for the help of Willis Barnstone with the final stanza.

"Let the Dead Bury Their Own" is a poem prompted by decades of water contamination at Camp Lejeune, North Carolina, the subsequent cover-up of its impact, and the heroes who led the advocacy charge for victims: Jerry Ensimger, USMC (Ret.), Mike Partain, and CAP representatives who continue to fight for health care coverage for survivors.

The italicized portions and the inspiration for "Generational Memory Theory" comes from the December 2013 BBC news article "'Memories' Pass Between Generations" by James Gallagher.

AEHF-1 stands for Advanced Extremely High Frequency 1; this satellite's story was documented in Justin Ray's Space.com article "Fight to Save US Military Satellite Ends in Remarkable Rescue."

"Pentimento" refers to "an underlying image in a painting, as an earlier painting, part of a painting, or original draft, that shows through, usually when the top layer of paint has become transparent with age." The line "things lost to the flood" comes from Lorine Niedecker, and "Rain fell in an empty town" comes from Karen Volkman.

"Interior with Sudden Joy" gets its title from the 1951 Dorothea Tanning painting.

"Full as Opera" is a construction in the poetry of Emily Dickinson and was written in light of Joseph Cornell's untitled ("Bébé Marie") assemblage.

Alice Neel's 1980 self-portrait inspires "Thoughts Before Self-Portrait."

"Dead reckoning" is the process of determining location based on a fix rather than using celestial navigation.

ACKNOWLEDGMENTS

I am grateful to the editors who published these poems in earlier versions:

"Restitution for Chaos," "Self-Portrait as Venus," "Wistful Theory" and
    "Dead Reckoning" in *The Northern Virginia Review*
"Nocebo Theory" and "Predilection" in *Sin City Poetry Review*
"Pink Pill Theory," "Chinook Theory," and "Maternal Theory" in *So to
    Speak: a feminist journal of art and literature*
"Inaccurate Theory" in *CALYX: A Journal of Art and Literature by Women*
"Theory for the Living" in *The Cortland Review*
"Gentle Obsessions" and "Overleveraged Theory" in *RUST + MOTH*
"Let the Dead Bury Their Own" on the blog for *The Philadelphia Review
    of Books*
"Generational Memory Theory" in *Snapdragon: A Journal of Art and
    Healing*
"How to Apologize" in *District Lit*
"Some Theory" as "Materiality" in *Yalobusha Review*
"Marathon" and "Full as Opera" in *Clade Song*
"Intimacy Theory" in *Still: A Journal*
"Interior with Sudden Joy" in *Sugared Water*
"Corporeal Theories" in *Hermeneutic Chaos*
"Miscarriage as a Landline Phone Call" in *Rogue Agent*

***

"Sister," "Pentimento," and "Thoughts Before Self-Portrait" received a
    2008 Dorothy Sargent Rosenberg Memorial Prize.
"*Via Negativa*" was published as a broadside by Black Orchid Designs, an
    imprint of ELJ publications.
"Gentle Obsessions" also appeared in *Emily: An Anthology* a Dickinson-
    inspired published by Porkbelly Press.

***

Finishing Line Press published *My Mine*, a limited-edition chapbook of the
following poems in 2015:

"Hypothesis," "Theory for the Living," "Predilection," "Pentimento,"
"Marathon," "Wistful Theory," "Sister," "Self-Portrait as Venus," "*No
Theory*," "Thoughts Before Self-Portrait," "Full as Opera," "Grief Theory,"
"Inaccurate Theory," "Some Theory," and "Intimacy Theory."

Thanks to the Vermont Studio Center, Virginia Center for the Creative Arts,
and Woodlawn & Frank Lloyd Wright's Pope-Leighey House for the space to
write many of these poems, to George Mason University for the Thesis Fel-
lowship, and to Northern Virginia Community College for the President's
Sabbatical Award, which afforded me the time away from teaching to com-
plete this collection.

Thanks to Kathleen Wheaton and Washington Writers' Publishing House,
the collective of writers who selected this book, and to Jean Feldman for
funding the award. Special thanks to Holly Karapetkova, Robert Herschbach,
and Sid Gold for their feedback during the editorial process and to Patric
Pepper and Barbara Shaw for their help turning the manuscript into a book,
to Meg Reid for designing the cover, and to John Kelly for painting and al-
lowing me to use the cover image.

This book would not exist without Alan Michael Parker's invitation to play
in the sandbox that has most shaped my life; I am forever in his debt. I am
grateful to my former teachers and mentors including Tony Abbott, Cynthia
Lewis, Randy Nelson, Alan Michael Parker, Aliki Barnstone, Claudia Keelan,
Jennifer Atkinson, Zofia Burr, Eric Pankey, Susan Tichy, and my graduate
school comrades at University of Nevada, Las Vegas and George Mason Uni-
versity. Eric Pankey and the Heritage Workshop participants provided gener-
ous feedback.

I am grateful to Bill Miller for his work in support of literary endeavors in Fairfax. Thanks, Sisters, for your Sunday company and thoughts on the most recent of these poems. Thanks, Erin Elizabeth Smith and all of the Bees; I am grateful for every word of support and for the treasured Marianne Moore book you replaced post-flood. Thanks, Brandon, Kiley, Julie, Stacey, and Susan for receiving earlier versions of the manuscript and making thoughtful suggestions. Thanks, Noah Chiles, for reading with enthusiasm.

Mary Jo Bang, Marilyn Chin, Sally Keith, James Kimbrell, Jean Valentine, and Kevin Young wrote the books that made me want to write this book. I am grateful for their work with elegy, which provided me vital company.

To the community of runners whose nods, waves, and hugs kept me going during the hard days while I sorted through these ideas and voice-recorded early versions mid-run, to those with whom I have shared miles, and to Oana who helped me run this year, post-injury: thank you.

To Mom with love for reading to me and helping me write stories before I could do so on my own: every image here is a seed you planted. I am grateful.

To my family: Mom, Jennifer, Jason, Mason, Jackson, Rosie, Jerry, Alissa, Hannah, Mary Love, Megan, the Foremans, and the Caccamos: there is no greater gift than your love and support. Adam, Brian, Cara, Caleb, Carey, Christian, Christina, Damon, embry, Gail, Hayib, Indigo, Jen, James, Joe, Josh, Kevin, Kiley, Leslie, Ray, Sara, Team Cran, Veronica, and Yara deserve special thanks for their wonder.

To those who would be cheering the loudest: Dad, Paul, Anna. I hear you.

This book and everything else is for John; thank you for being my Team.

CPSIA information can be obtained
at www.ICGtesting.com
Printed in the USA
LVOW03s1731310717
543262LV00004B/555/P